TaeKwonDo - The Art

TAEKWONDO
Fun
Black and White edition
ACTIVITY BOOK

By Alex Man

Match the Taekwondo techniques

Which of the drawings match?

Popsicle sticks Taekwondo theater.

Color, cut, paste and have fun.

Popsicle sticks Taekwondo theater.

Color, cut, paste and have fun.

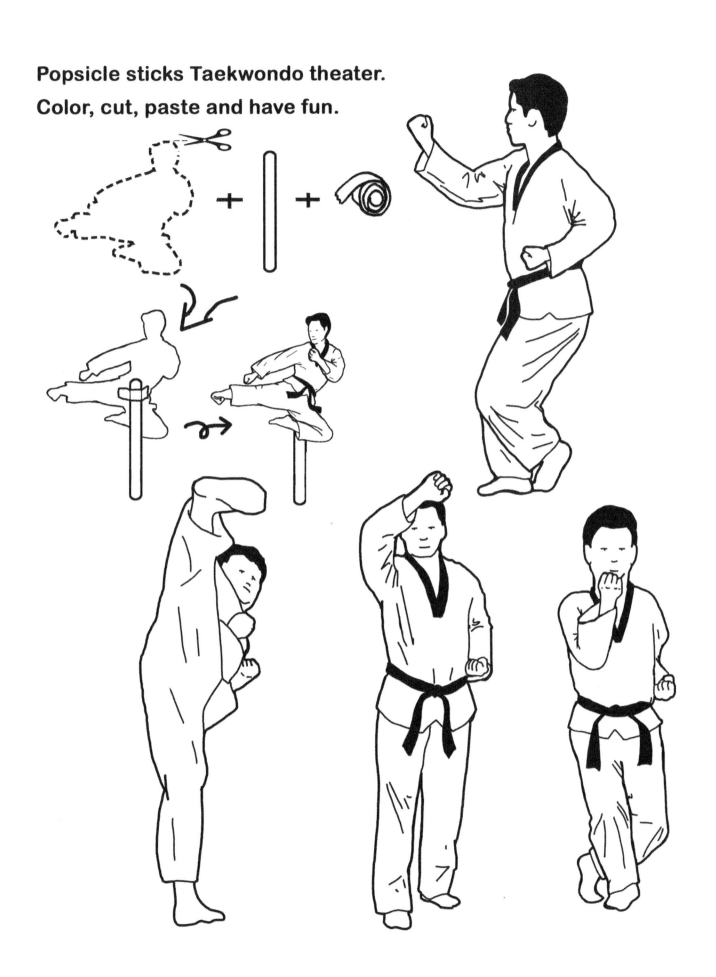

Jumping Turning Side Kick

Breaking Board

Instructions: color and cut the bookmarks.
Tip: for the bookmarks to last, laminate or paste them onto a cardboard. Enjoy reading!

1. Blue   2. Light blue   3. Red   4. Green   5. Gray

6. Black   7. Light brown   8. Any color you like

9. White

Find the differences (hint: there are 15 differences to be found)

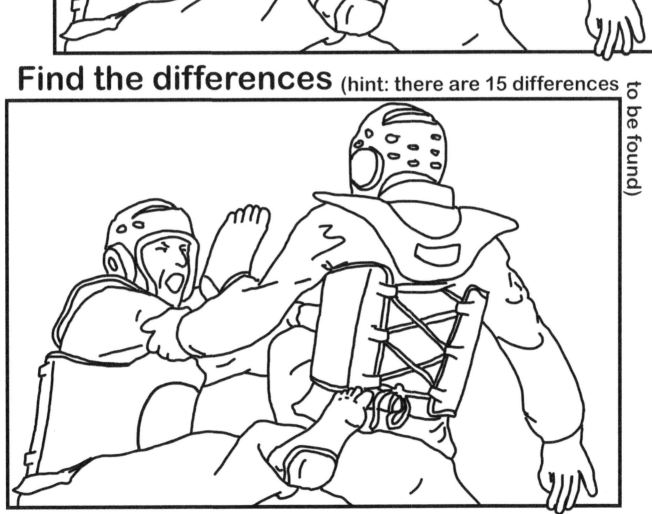

Tae

Kwon

Do

Ax Kick

MIDDLE BLOCK

Color and Enjoy

Color the belts and find which one is getting to the Taekwondo competitor.

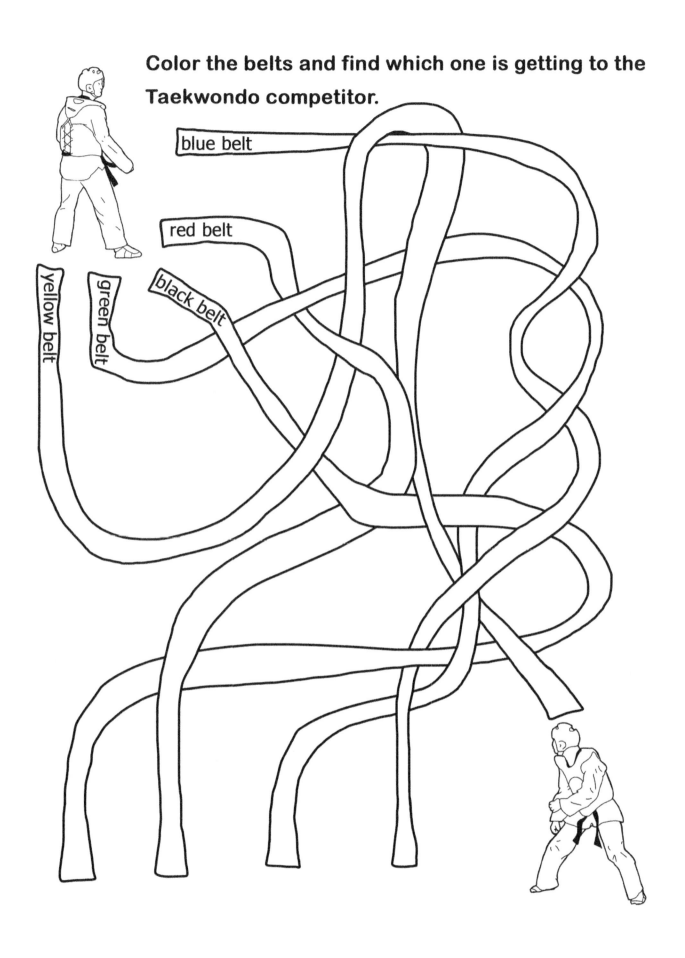

blue belt

red belt

yellow belt

green belt

black belt

Elbow Strike

Color and Enjoy

High block

Knife-hand
low block

Middle block

Knife-hand middle block

Single knife-hand block

Low block

How many Blocks, Kicks, and Punches can you find?
Blocks _____, Kicks _____, Punches _____.

Crescent Kick to the Target

Spear-hand Strike

(Front Stance)

Match the Taekwondo techniques to their silhouette

Tic- tac- toe

The goal of Tic-tac-toe is to get three in a row.
The first player is known as X (X block)
and the second is O (bull block).
Players alternate placing Xs and Os on the
game board until either opponent has three
in a row (vertical, horizontal or oblique)
all nine squares are filled.

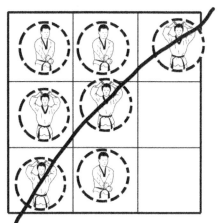

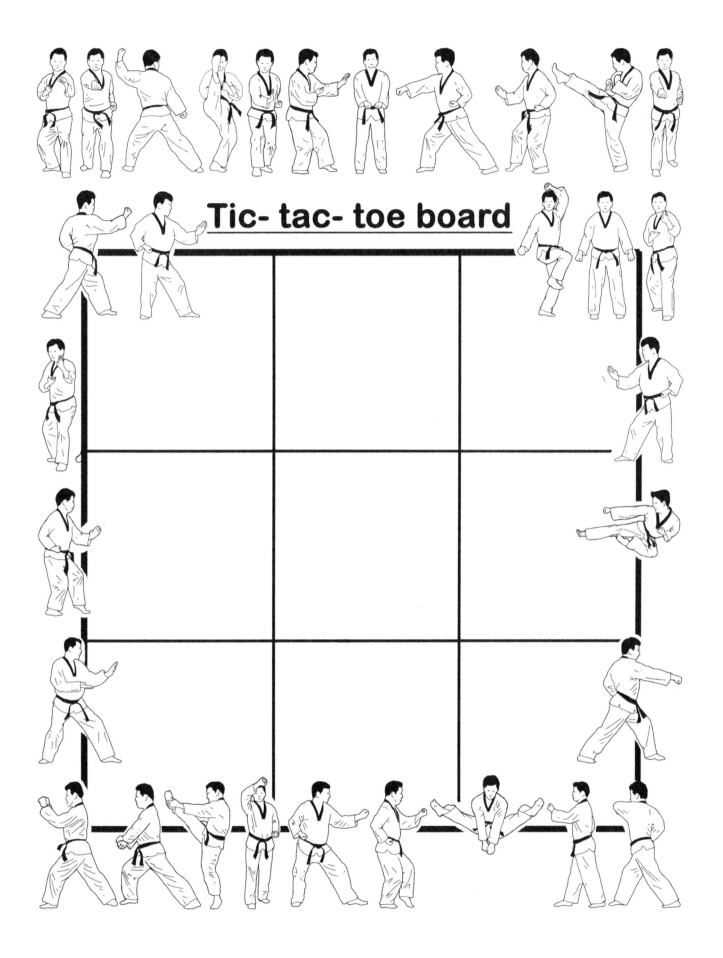

Tic- tac- toe board

Crescent kick

Spinning hook kick

Roundhouse kick

Front kick

Pushing kick

Side kick

Axe kick

Find
the
differences

(hint: there are
10 differences
to be found)

Use the grid as a guide to draw the Side Kick.

Help the young student to get to the Dojang (Taekwondo gym).

Instructions: color and cut the bookmarks.
Tip: for the bookmarks to last, laminate or paste them onto a cardboard. Enjoy reading!

Closed stance

Back stance

Walking stance

Ready stance

Front stance

Horse-riding stance

Use the grid
as a guide
to draw the
Taekwondo sparring.

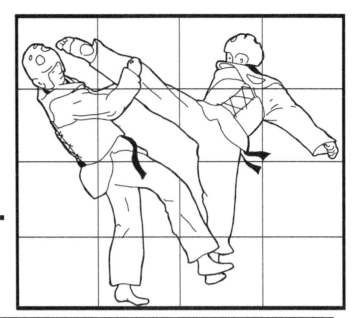

k	e	i	a	e	h	u	e	b	r	s	c	p	y	t	a	e
h	i	g	h	b	l	o	c	k	o	r	e	a	u	h	s	z
k	d	c	n	a	e	e	n	d	e	a	v	o	r	n	e	g
d	n	d	k	c	d	v	g	j	r	p	t	a	i	j	c	v
t	w	p	i	k	i	h	a	p	k	a	y	r	w	s	p	h
s	t	o	p	s	e	l	f	d	e	f	e	n	s	e	p	d
r	a	o	l	t	c	q	t	b	t	w	l	j	i	r	d	e
g	e	m	r	a	g	i	u	h	o	l	s	u	d	f	s	u
f	k	s	h	n	i	y	p	p	b	w	n	x	e	a	l	m
v	w	a	p	c	o	b	y	l	a	u	m	p	k	e	f	i
j	o	e	p	e	i	t	z	f	i	s	t	g	i	s	q	f
i	n	a	p	t	c	r	r	v	t	n	k	k	c	u	b	e
c	d	b	f	a	i	t	h	f	u	l	e	r	k	p	h	f
p	o	s	a	e	y	r	e	a	d	y	s	t	a	n	c	e
k	n	i	f	e	h	a	n	d	y	s	u	o	r	y	f	d

kick	side kick	fist	punch
high block	knife hand	ready stance	bow
back stance	poomsae	taekwondo	kihap
self defense	respect	power	korea
discipline	faithful	endeavor	

Dear reader,
Thank you so much for purchasing my book,
I hope you enjoyed it.
I will appreciate it if you can leave a review on Amazon.
Hope to see you soon.
Alex

Printed in Great Britain
by Amazon

40000517R00037